My State
MARYLAND

By Christina Earley

TABLE OF CONTENTS

A Crabtree Seedlings Book

Crabtree Publishing

crabtreebooks.com

School-to-Home Support for Caregivers and Teachers

This book helps children grow by letting them practice reading. Here are a few guiding questions to help the reader build his or her comprehension skills. Possible answers appear in red.

Before Reading:

- What do I know about Maryland?
    - *I know that Maryland is a state.*
    - *I know that Maryland is historic.*

- What do I want to learn about Maryland?
    - *I want to learn which famous people were born in Maryland.*
    - *I want to learn what the state flag looks like.*

During Reading:

- What have I learned so far?
    - *I have learned that Annapolis is the state capital of Maryland.*
    - *I have learned that Great Falls is on the Potomac River.*

- I wonder why...
    - *I wonder why the state flower is the black-eyed Susan.*
    - *I wonder why there are wild horses on Assateague Island.*

After Reading:

- What did I learn about Maryland?
    - *I have learned that you can fish at Calvert Cliffs State Park.*
    - *I have learned that the state bird is the Baltimore oriole.*

- Read the book again and look for the glossary words.
    - *I see the word **capital** on page 6, and the word **produces** on page 11. The other glossary words are found on pages 22 and 23.*

MARYLAND
Hi! My name is Ruby. Welcome to Maryland!
CHESAPEAKE
NATIONAL AQUARIUM

I live in Ellicott City. There are many **historic** buildings in my city.

Ellicott City has the oldest **remaining** railway station in the U.S.!

Maryland is in the **mid-Atlantic** United States. The **capital** is Annapolis.

Fun Fact: Baltimore is the largest city in Maryland.

The state bird is the Baltimore oriole.

The black-eyed
Susan is the
state flower.

We grow a lot of corn in Maryland. Some of it is used to make corn on the cob.

Fun Fact: Maryland **produces** 700,000 tons (635,000 metric tons) of sweet corn a year.

My state flag shows two **coats of arms**. They belong to two families that were important in Maryland's history.

My family enjoys watching the Baltimore Orioles play baseball.

I like to visit Great Falls. I enjoy watching the water rush over the waterfalls.

Fun Fact: Great Falls is a series of waterfalls and rapids on the Potomac River.

I ride roller coasters with my family at Six Flags America.

I like to visit Assateague Island and see the wild horses that live there.

Author Frederick Douglass was born in Maryland. Swimmer Michael Phelps was also born in Maryland.

Fun Fact: Activist Harriet Tubman was born in Dorchester County, Maryland.

I like to go fishing at Calvert Cliffs State Park.

I enjoy learning about American history at Fort McHenry National Monument and Historic Shrine.

Glossary

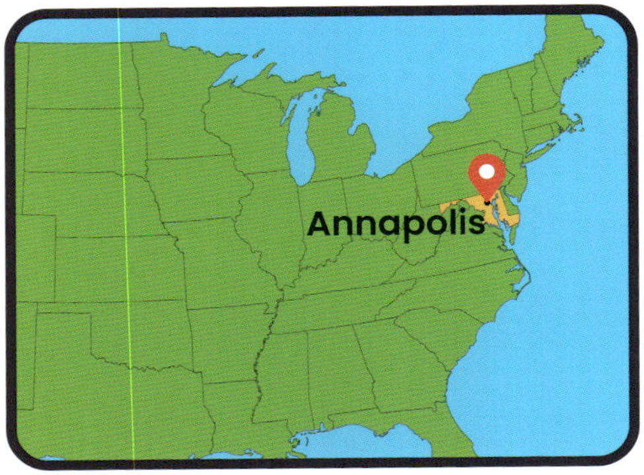

capital (cap-ih-tuhl): The city or town where the government of a country, state, or province is located

coat of arms (coht uv armz): A special group of pictures, usually shown on a shield

historic (hi-stor-ik): Something that is important in history

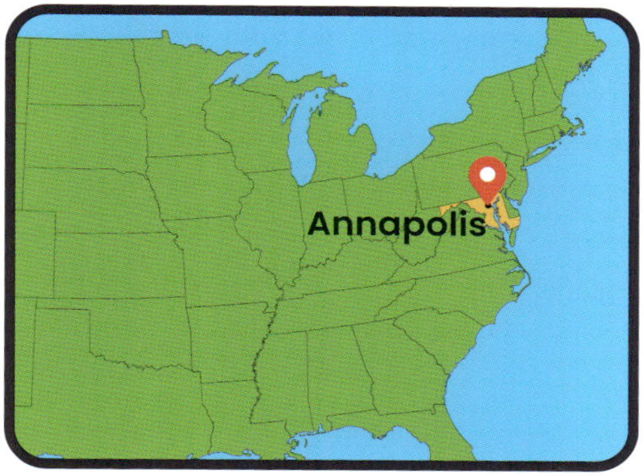

mid-Atlantic (mid-at-lan-tik): The northeastern area of the United States

produces (pruh-doos-es): Makes or grows something for sale or use

remaining (ri-meyn-ing): Still existing

Index

About the Author

Christina Earley lives in sunny South Florida with her husband and son. She enjoys traveling around the United States and learning about different historical places. Her hobbies include hiking, yoga, and baking.

Written by: Christina Earley
Designed and Illustrated by: Bobbie Houser
Series Development: James Earley
Proofreader: Melissa Boyce
Educational Consultant: Marie Lemke M.Ed.

Photographs:
Alamy: Hemis: p. 4, 22
LOC: p. 18 left; p. 19
Newscom: Joe Robbins/Icon Sportswire 573: p. 13
Shutterstock: Jon Bilous: cover; Bill Chizek: p. 3; Rosemarie Mosteller: p. 5, 23; Volina: p. 6, 22-23; Sean Pavone: p. 7; Shutterstock: p. 8; Katie Manchester: p. 9; chanwangrong: p. 10-11; Ken Felepchuk: p. 11, 23; railway fx: p. 12, 22; Andrei Medvedev: p. 14-15; MarkVanDykePhotography: p. 15; Cvandyke: p. 16; Wendy Farrington: p. 17; Salty View: p. 18 right; Jon Bilous: p. 20; Melissa A. Woolf: p. 21

Crabtree Publishing

crabtreebooks.com 800-387-7650

Printed in the U.S.A./072023/CG20230214

Published in Canada
Crabtree Publishing
616 Welland Avenue
St. Catharines, Ontario
L2M 5V6

Published in the United States
Crabtree Publishing
347 Fifth Avenue
Suite 1402-145
New York, New York, 10016

Library and Archives Canada Cataloguing in Publication
Available at Library and Archives Canada

Library of Congress Cataloging-in-Publication Data
Available at the Library of Congress

Hardcover: 978-1-0398-0519-4
Paperback: 978-1-0398-0551-4
Ebook (pdf): 978-1-0398-0615-3
Epub: 978-1-0398-0583-5